The 1984 Election in Historical Perspective

by
William E. Leuchtenburg

THE SEVENTH

𝕮harles 𝕰dmondson 𝕳istorical 𝕷ectures

Baylor University • Waco, Texas
March 4 and 5, 1985

MARKHAM PRESS FUND
WACO, TEXAS

This volume is the twentieth volume published by the Markham Press Fund of Baylor University Press, established in memory of Dr. L. N. and Princess Finch Markham of Longview, Texas, by their daughters, Mrs. R. Matt Dawson of Waco, Texas, and Mrs. B. Reid Clanton of Longview, Texas.

The Charles Edmondson Historical Lecture Series, Number 7.

Rufus B. Spain, general editor

Publication of this series of lectures is made possible by a special grant from Dr. E. Bud Edmondson of Longview, Texas.

Library of Congress Catalog Card Number: 86-72071
International Standard Book Number: 0-918954-45-2

Printed in the United States of America by the Baylor University Press, Waco, Texas 76798.

This book was set in Hanover, and was printed and bound by Baylor University Press.

FOREWORD

In 1975 Dr. E. Bud Edmondson of Longview, Texas, began an endowment fund at Baylor University to honor his father, Mr. Charles S. B. Edmondson. Dr. Edmondson's intent was to have the proceeds from the fund used to bring to the University outstanding historians who could synthesize, interpret, and communicate history in such a way as to make the past relevant to the present generation.

Baylor University and the Waco community are grateful to Dr. Edmondson for his generosity in establishing the CHARLES EDMONDSON HISTORICAL LECTURES.

Dr. William E. Leuchtenburg, the seventh Edmondson Lecturer, focuses on recent developments in the American two-party system, as understood from analyses of its past. Lecture I reviews our experiences from the Civil War to the New Deal, and Lecture II covers the period from FDR to Ronald Reagan.

****

The views expressed in these lectures are those of the author and do not necessarily reflect the position of Baylor University or of the Markham Press Fund.

****

Although the Charles Edmondson Historical Lectures have been presented annually at Baylor University since 1978, they have not always been available for publication by the Markham Press Fund. Therefore, while this volume represents the fifth of the lectures to be published, they were the seventh presented in the lecture series. A list of previous lectures appears at the end of this work.

3

FROM THE CIVIL WAR
TO THE NEW DEAL

As we think back on the 1984 election, we understandably concentrate our attention on the issues and candidates of that November Tuesday. But when the American people went to the polls, most of the votes cast responded not only to contemporary concerns but to historical forces, some more than a century old. In the 1980s a young woman in a New Hampshire village will attend social studies classes, give a fair hearing to both parties, wonder in her own mind what she is going to do, and when the time comes will cast a solid vote for the Republican party—in good part because of a quarrel over the Kansas-Nebraska Act about which she may never even have heard. At the same time, a young man in Detroit will examine the records of the candidates, score the televised debates, and then vote the straight Democratic ticket because of benefits his grandparents received from Franklin Roosevelt's New Deal, about which he may be only dimly aware.

You might suppose that every four years the electorate makes up its mind afresh on the basis of which candidates are running, but that is not usually what happens. Studies of electoral behavior have shown that, to an extraordinary extent, votes are cast in keeping with settled traditions and that, over a period of many years, one party is dominant. In the twentieth century, there have been two such eras—the first three decades, when the Republicans carried on the superiority they had established in the nineteenth century, and the years from the Great Depression to the recent period when the Democrats have been the majority party.

How does it happen that one party can prevail for so long? Because of a phenomenon called "party identification." Most people come to regard themselves as either Democrats or Republicans and they maintain that allegiance election after election, often through an entire lifetime. The situation in

America is much like that described for England by Gilbert and Sullivan:

How nature always does contrive
That every boy and every gal,
That's born into the world alive,
Is either a little Liberal,
Or else a little Conservative!

How do you get a party identification? Here an analogy may be helpful. How do you become a Methodist? You might imagine that at a certain age a young man or woman begins studying theology and visits a series of religious services—at a synagogue, a Baptist church, a Moslem mosque—and finally decides that he or she likes Methodism best. But that is, of course, not at all what happens. You are a Methodist because you are born a Methodist. Some people, of course, go through an experience of conversion later in life, but not many. Most of us are Methodists (or Baptists or Jews or Catholics or any other faith) because our parents are. In like manner do we fall heir to our party identification. As Elizabeth Hardwick writes in one of her novels, "So many...children...from the day of their birth are growing up to be their parents. Look at the voting records, inherited like flat feet."

Many will instinctively resist such a conception, for it may be thought to indicate that political behavior is altogether pre-determined and irrational. In fact, there are very good reasons—of class, ethnicity, geography—for why party systems develop and why they endure. Furthermore, though the religious analogue is useful, it is somewhat mischievous, since political attachments are considerably more fluid than commitments to a particular creed. Nonetheless, many do find it almost as hard to abandon the party of their upbringing as to change their form of worship. Indeed, it usually requires a cataclysmic event to realign voters into a new party system, and even when a cataclysm like that of the Great Depression strikes, the vast majority of citizens will continue to hold fast to their ancestral loyalties.

For millions of Americans over the past 130 years, the party they identified with was determined by the accident of where they were born. Until recently, it seemed as natural for a

Mississippian to vote Democratic as it did for a Vermonter to vote Republican. The sectional divisions of the twentieth century—divisions that still may be discerned, however dimly, in our own day—go back to the era of Civil War and Reconstruction. Decades later, the country continued to bear the marks of the cleavages of the struggle over slavery and secession. The Republicans were powerful in the northern countryside that had been the stronghold of the Union, the Democrats in the states of the former Confederacy. The exceptions are particularly illuminating. In the South, pockets of Union sentiment during the Civil War, especially mountain areas that rejected secession in 1861, persist as enclaves of Republicanism to this very day.

Take a look, for example, at what happens in 1936. The country is in the seventh year of the Great Depression and appears to be wholly preoccupied with economic survival. Most Americans give their support to the Democratic candidate, Franklin D. Roosevelt, who is especially popular in the South. The nation is preoccupied with modern problems of mass unemployment, and Bull Run and Chickamauga are far in the past. Yet that year people in the old anti-Confederate sections of the southern Appalachians vote 89 percent for the Republican Alf Landon at a time when most of the South is going overwhelmingly to FDR. In an age of breadlines and sitdown strikes, voters are still reflecting the passions over John Brown's raid.

Even after World War II, American politics continued to show the effects of nineteenth-century controversies. That was a time of modern issues such as the cold war and the atomic bomb. So how do people behave when they go to the polls, ostensibly with these matters in mind? A voting study found, "If one plots on the map of Indiana clusters of underground railroad stations and points at which Union authorities had difficulties in drafting troops, he separates, on the whole, Republican and Democratic counties [in America today]."

For a number of years I wrote the presidential vote analysis on election night for NBC, first for Huntley and Brinkley, then for John Chancellor. I would arrive at the big studio in the RCA building in Manhattan at about five in the afternoon, knowing that the early reports would be presented on the seven

7

o'clock evening news and that I would need to have copy ready
before then, even though I had only scattered returns to work
with. In trying to find a meaningful pattern, I would always
watch for towns like Evansville, Indiana, which still reflected
the sympathies of settlers from the Confederacy who had
crossed the Ohio, even if few of the descendants of the
Copperheads in Evansville in the 1960s or the 1970s could have
told you who Jefferson Davis was.

Many of the votes cast for the Republicans in 1984 derived
from affinities formed not in the past generation, but during
the long period when the Republicans were the country's
dominant party. From 1860 to 1932, only two Democrats entered
the White House, both with less than a popular majority.
Otherwise, in that long stretch of seventy-two years, the
Republicans prevailed. Leaders of the Grand Old Party claimed
that their organization was nothing less than the party of the
union, the party of Abraham Lincoln, the nation's savior, the
party that won the Civil War. For a generation, the Republicans
had a simple appeal to voters in the North: "Vote the way you
shot."

The electoral strength of the Republican party reflected the
pre-Civil War divisions between New England anti-slavery
voters and the slavocracy. The Republicans usually held New
England and the entire New England belt of migration sweeping
west across the plains to Oregon. So tenacious were these
associations that Iowa did not elect a Democratic governor until
1932, and in its long history Vermont did not choose a
Democratic governor until 1962—much more than a century
after the Democratic party was founded.

In the West, voters hailed the Republicans as the party of
the Homestead Act, the party that criss-crossed the trans-
Mississippi country with railroads, and the party of national
expansion. When in 1874, one Alfred Packer was convicted of
killing five Colorado prospectors and eating them, the judge,
at the end of his trial, said: "There were only six Democrats
in all of Hinsdale County and you ate five of them. I sentence
you to hang—as a warning against further reducing the
Democratic population in this county." (As it happens, he
escaped hanging and to this day the student cafeteria at the
University of Colorado is called, in his honor, the Alfred E.

8

Packer Grill.) Though the West has shifted from time to time since then, it has been a bastion of the Republicans in recent years, in part because of the strength of loyalties first developed in that earlier period.

The geographical distribution of the electorate had profound ideological consequences. New England and the New England belt of migration were preponderantly Protestant, and throughout its history the Republican party has found its staunchest following among northern evangelical Protestants, including immigrants whose "Anglo-Saxon" origins lay in Great Britain, Germany, and Scandinavia. Consequently, the Republicans have always been aligned with those forces more favorable to a Protestant outlook, while the Democrats, in 1928 and 1960, have been the only major party to nominate a Catholic for the presidency. It was wholly in keeping with this tradition that in 1984 again the Democrats had a Catholic on their national ticket.

As yet another outgrowth of the era of Civil War and Reconstruction, the Republicans for a long time could count upon most black voters to remain wedded to the party of the Great Emancipator. The black leader Frederick Douglass said: "The Republican party is the ship; all else is the sea." In 1896, 90 percent of black votes in Chicago went to the Republicans, and as late as the 1920s, only 5 percent of Chicago's blacks thought of themselves as Democrats. Even in 1932, though blacks suffered cruelly in the Great Depression with the Republicans in office, a sizeable majority of black voters supported Herbert Hoover, the GOP candidate. The Republicans have never reconciled themselves to the loss of the black vote in the past half century, and they continue today to try to persuade black citizens that their natural home is the party of Abraham Lincoln, so far without much success.

The Republicans had one final advantage. With their great attraction to old-stock Americans in the New England belt which prided itself on its role as the guardian and carrier of culture, they regarded themselves as the party of the better elements and the spokesmen for the Yankee enlightenment of Emerson and Whittier. In a speech on the fiftieth anniversary of the Republican party, John Hay wryly attributed to the party "all the good things of the half century, except, possibly, the

9

introduction of antiseptic surgery." Through much of its history, people have thought of the Republican party as the naturally ruling group in America. As Mr. Dooley once observed: "History always vindicates the Democrats, but never in their lifetime. They see the truth first, but the trouble is that nothing is ever officially true till a Republican sees it."

Furthermore, if the Republicans claimed to be the carriers of culture, the Democrats were reputed to be the party of saloon keepers. In 1872, when the editor Horace Greeley, a lifelong Republican, ran for the Presidency as a Liberal Republican, he needed Democratic support to win, but he was hard put to defend some of his published statements which now came back to embarrass him. "I never *said* all Democrats were saloonkeepers," Greeley protested. "What I *said* was that all saloonkeepers were *Democrats*." Probably the most famous story of the period is of the man who shouted through the window of a city council meeting in New York City, "Alderman, your saloon is on fire"—and thereby emptied the chamber. In addition, in the North during the Civil War era and afterwards, the Democratic party labored under the severe disadvantage of being regarded as the party of "the enemy." Outside of the South, few of the substantial people of the country were Democrats. Fred Howe recalls: "There was something unthinkable to me about being a Democrat—Democrats, Copperheads and atheists were persons whom one did not know socially. As a boy I did not play with their children." In the village of West Branch, Iowa, where Herbert Hoover grew up, there was only one Democrat—the town drunk.

To many Republicans, the Democratic party seemed almost illegitimate. Since a large number of Democrats opposed temperance laws, were devout Catholics, and had been Confederate sympathizers, the Democrats were, as a Republican clergyman was indiscreet enough to say, the party of "Rum, Romanism, and Rebellion." James Thurber, writing of his Midwest boyhood, remembered that "youngsters grew up in the vague belief that Democrats kept Confederate flags in their attics and were probably guilty of living in sin and responsible for the sinking of the Maine." In the eyes of Republicans, indeed, the Democrats continued to be the party of heresy and even of treason from the Copperhead Clement Vallandigham in the

10

1860s to Alger Hiss in the 1950s. As recently as 1984, the Republicans depicted the Democrats as hostile to a strong national defense and suspiciously soft on communism.

To this day, many Americans continue to view the Republicans as the more respectable party, the party of old stock piety, and think of the Democrats as somehow less "American." It is that perception of the two parties that may sway the vote of the hypothetical young woman from the small New Hampshire town, and the Republicans know how to exploit it. At Dallas at their national convention, they presented themselves as America's party and left the impression that no athlete earned a gold medal at the Olympics who was not a card-carrying member of the GOP.

But Republican votes are not the only ones predisposed. For the past half century and more even larger numbers of citizens have identified themselves with the Democrats. And just as the sentiments of the New Hampshire woman came originally from developments associated with catastrophe—that of the Civil War—so does the identification of the hypothetical young man from Detroit derive from a catastrophic event: the Great Depression that began with the Wall Street crash of 1929.

The depression had a calamitous impact on the political fortunes of the GOP. Until 1929 the Republicans had been thought of not only as the party of the union but as the party of prosperity. Their real era of predominance had not begun until the 1890s when they were able to take advantage of popular resentment toward the Democrats who were in power during the hard times of the Panic of 1893. For a generation, the Republicans had identified themselves with the promise of abundance—from the full dinner pail of McKinley in 1896 to the two-cars-in-every-garage of Hoover in 1928. But the Wall Street crash and the ensuing depression made a mockery of that reputation. In just three years under the Republican Hoover, national income was cut in half, and one-third of the working force became unemployed. The countryside was devastated, as wheat prices fell to the lowest level since the reign of Charles II, and industrial America was ravaged. In the 1920s manufacturers of locomotives sold American railroads an average of 1300 locomotives a year; in 1932 they sold none. In the coal region of Illinois, the town of Coello had a population of 1,350; the

11

total number of people employed in that town was two. Not for thirty years would New York City build a new hotel or a new theater.

To get a sense of the extent of unemployment in these years, imagine one hundred thousand people in a huge football stadium. And imagine that as they leave the stadium each person is handed a slip saying that he or she is fired. Imagine that the following week another one hundred thousand enter the stadium and that as they file out, each of them is given a pink slip. And imagine that happening each successive week for fifty-two weeks of the year. For three straight years. You will then have approximated the totals of jobless in the United States in early 1933, at a time when the working force was less than half what it is today.

Few classes seemed to have cheerier prospects than the one that was graduated from college in the spring of 1929, but many in that class would find no work in 1930, 1931, 1932, 1933. Indeed, full employment would not be restored until 1942, an appalling thirteen years after the crash, and by then many of the young men of the class of 1929 would be in uniform. Those of the class of 1929 who survived the war would not know their first peacetime prosperity until 1946, by which time they would be about thirty-eight years old.

The mass unemployment took a terrible toll. Thomas Wolfe reported on the winter of 1930-31 in New York: "I saw half naked wretches sitting on park benches at three in the morning in a freezing rain and sleet: often I saw a man and a woman huddled together with their arms around each other for warmth, and with sodden newspapers, rags, or anything they could find over their shoulders." At the end of 1931, a Philadelphia relief authority announced: "We have unemployment in every third house. It is almost like the visitation of death to the households of the Egyptians at the time of the escape of the Jews from Egypt." For some groups, discrimination added to the already awful burden. The city of Houston announced: "Applications [for relief] are not taken from unemployed Mexican or colored families. They are being asked to shift for themselves."

There was bound to be a political reckoning, and any party in power during the disaster—in Australia, Labor; in the United States, the Republicans—would have to pay the price. In the language of political scientists, the Republican party had been "deauthorized" by the Great Depression. But Hoover's ideological rigidity, his cold personality, and his insistence that people were being cared for when they clearly were not augmented the party's difficulties. There were no limits to what was said about Hoover. It was reported that dogs took an instinctive dislike to him; that 'Erbie was an agent of British interests; even "that he was the mastermind behind the kidnapping and murder" of the Lindbergh baby. When the Republican campaign train rolled into Detroit, with its huge armies of jobless, one writer has noted, "the men on it heard a hoarse, rhythmic chant rising from thousands of throats; for a moment they had hopes of an enthusiastic reception—and then they made out the words of the chant: 'Hang Hoover! Hang Hoover! Hang Hoover!' " By the end of the campaign, the President looked, it was said, like a "walking corpse." One telegram to him summed up the national mood: "Vote for Roosevelt and make it unanimous."

On Election Night, Hoover awaited news of the returns at his home on the Stanford campus, and the issue was not long in doubt. Not for eighty years had there been such an avalanche of Democratic ballots. Strongholds that the Republicans had maintained since before the Civil War were overwhelmed. In the first national election since the crash, Hoover went down to defeat and Franklin D. Roosevelt, carrying every state south and west of Pennsylvania, became the first Democrat since Franklin Pierce to enter the White House with a majority of the popular vote. The Republican party system had been shattered, and in the only realignment in this century, a new Democratic party system began to take its place.

Four years later Roosevelt did even better. As he toured the country in 1936, the response of crowds startled veterans of previous campaigns. In 1932 the country had voted less for FDR than against Hoover. "Mr. Roosevelt was no great popular idol during the presidential campaign of 1932," wrote one correspondent. "Vast crowds came out to look at him eagerly, hopefully. They liked him but went away still skeptical." But in the intervening years Roosevelt had transformed the Democratic party, hitherto an organization addicted to localism, into an instrumentality of national purpose. He identified the

13

Democrats with a bold legislative agenda, a distinctive public philosophy, and a commitment to activism. By the end of his first term, many Americans had come to view the President as one who was assiduously attentive to their welfare. In the 1936 campaign, he heard people cry out, "He saved my home," "He gave me a job." At Bridgeport, Connecticut, he rode past signs saying, "Thank God for Roosevelt," and in the Denver freight yards a message scrawled in chalk on the side of a boxcar read, "Roosevelt Is My Friend."

When in November 1936 the first election returns reached the President at his home at Hyde Park, he leaned back, blew a smoke ring, and said, "Wow!" New Haven, Connecticut, had gone to FDR by 15,000—the earliest indication of the power of Roosevelt's urban coalition. Through the night the wire services ticked the tidings of a landslide victory. The President's twenty-eight million votes set a new mark. Nor had anyone ever equalled FDR's more than eleven million plurality. Even more impressive was the tally in electoral votes, as he swept every state but Maine and Vermont. It used to be said that as Maine goes, so goes the nation. Now it was said, as Maine goes, so goes Vermont. Roosevelt's electoral triumph was the greatest since James Monroe had won in 1820 with no opposition, and the President carried so many of his party into office with him that in Congress a number of Democrats had to sit on the Republican side of the aisle. Afterwards, one writer stated, "If the outcome of his election hasn't taught you Republicans not to meddle in politics, I don't know what will." FDR himself was jubilant. "I knew I should have gone to Maine and Vermont," he said.

The Great Depression and the New Deal encouraged millions of first-time voters, especially those from families that had come to this country by the millions from southern and eastern Europe earlier in the century, to cast their lots with the Democrats as the party of compassion and of ideas, and tore numbers of Republicans loose from their moorings. In 1928, one couple christened their newborn son "Herbert Hoover Jones." Four years later they petitioned the court, "desiring to relieve the young man from the chagrin and mortification which he is suffering and will suffer," and asked that his name be changed—to Franklin D. Roosevelt Jones.

14

From the Great Depression to the 1980s, the Democrats have been the majority party in this country. That is to say, more Americans—from 1932 until 1984—have thought of themselves as Democrats than as Republicans. As a result, for more than half a century the Republicans have won control of Congress only twice. To put it another way, they have not held both houses of Congress for the last thirty years.

The Democratic coalition, the FDR coalition as it came to be called, had three components:

The first was the traditional source of Democratic power, the Solid South. In 1880, after the last of the federal troops was withdrawn from the South, the Democratic presidential candidate carried every state of the former Confederacy, and for the next sixty years, with rare exceptions, the Democrats entered each national campaign with the electoral votes of the southern states as good as already registered in their column. In the Deep South, the Republican party all but disappeared and national elections became a charade. On one occasion, Senator Cole Blease of South Carolina, noting that a total of little more than a thousand votes had been cast for the Republican presidential candidate in the entire state, said: "I do not know where he got them. I was astonished to know they were cast and shocked to know they were counted."

Throughout this period, southern whites—and until recently very few blacks voted in the South—cleaved to the Democratic party as the organization that from the pre-Civil War era onwards had preserved white supremacy. Their allegiance constituted a different version of "Vote the way you shot." That commitment was as strong in the Great Depression as it had been in the 1880s. There had been a defection in 1928, but in 1932 and, indeed, all four times that he ran, Roosevelt carried every state of the Solid South. In South Carolina in 1936 he rolled up a stunning proportion of the vote—more than 98½ percent.

Even after World War II, men with a lively sense of the struggles of the era of slavery and reconstruction wielded great influence in national affairs. I got a vivid confirmation of that reality at the 1952 Democratic national convention in Chicago when, to carry out an assignment in the fight over the credentials of the Mississippi and Arkansas delegations, I was required

15

to go on the convention floor where I stood directly under the rostrum and could look up at the face of the chairman of that stormy session. He was an unforgettable figure—the Speaker of the House, Sam Rayburn of Texas, a man with a bullet head, a forbidding glare, very much master of the situation. Here we were in the second half of the twentieth century, in the stockyards of a northern metropolis of two million people in the age of the cold war and the civil rights movement, and the presiding officer was a man who, a friend said, would "not in his lifetime forget Appomattox." For years, his office was adorned with pictures, all of the same man—Robert E. Lee. And on one occasion he declared: "As long as I honor the memory of the Confederate dead, and revere the gallant devotion of my Confederate father to the Southland, I will never vote for the electors of a party which sent the carpetbagger and the scalawag to the prostrate South with saber and sword."

The second element of the FDR coalition was the allegiance of lower income voters, many of them mobilized by the increasingly militant labor movement. If section was the hallmark of the era of Republican supremacy, social stratification has been the distinguishing mark of the modern Democratic party system. In 1936 Roosevelt received only 42 percent of the upper income share of the two-party vote, but 76 percent of lower income voters. He won 80 percent of the labor union vote, 84 percent of the ballots cast for the major parties by welfare recipients. This lower income component continued to be the characteristic feature of Democratic voting years after FDR's death. Even today, millions of Americans think of the Republicans as the hardhearted party of privilege, the Democrats as the generous party of the common man.

The third element of the Roosevelt coalition has been the strength of the Democrats among ethnic groups in the great cities. In 1936 FDR rolled up a plurality of well over a million votes in New York City, carried San Francisco by 3-1, Milwaukee by 4-1, in not a few places by cashing in on the traditional tendencies of the Irish. It had long been regarded as axiomatic that any good Irishman was a Democrat:

"Have you heard the news? John Danaher has become a Republican."

"It can't be true. I saw him at mass just last Sunday."

16

Most of the Irish were Catholics, and they resented the nativism and anti-Catholicism associated with the Republican party. Chiefly working-class, they felt a class antipathy to the Republican gentry. Concentrated in cities, they came into political and cultural conflicts with the rural pietistic Protestant supporters of the Republican party. In particular, they objected to the emphasis in the New England belt of Republicanism on the public enforcement of morals, especially with respect to temperance. Mr. Dooley, who reflected Irish skepticism of reformism, once commented on the American holiday of Thanksgiving: "Twas founded by the Puritans to give thanks for being preserved from the Indians, and we keep it to give thanks we are preserved from the Puritans."

In the age of Roosevelt, the Democrats increased their Irish-Catholic following, doing even better than they had in Al Smith's 1928 campaign, and expanded their appeal to other ethnic groups. In 1936, one prominent Catholic clergyman reported that "everybody in California is for Roosevelt, especially the nuns," while another cleric reckoned that 103 of the 106 bishops voted for the President. Jews, who admired FDR's liberal programs, his association with "Brain Trust" intellectuals, and his resistance to Hitler (in 1944, in Jewish neighborhoods in Brooklyn even Republican poll-watchers voted for Roosevelt), also gravitated to the Democrats. Still more conspicuously, blacks turned away from the party of Lincoln in 1936 and, in appreciation of the New Deal, cast their lots with the Democratic party where they have largely remained ever since.

In 1940 Roosevelt put this winning combination to a severe test by defying precedent to seek a third consecutive term. The Republicans magnified the risk by nominating not a humdrum candidate but the dynamic Wendell Willkie who said he was eager to take on "the Champ." Roosevelt sought to turn away this challenge by appearing in the garb of commander-in-chief of the armed services. One Republican Congressman grumbled, "Franklin Roosevelt is not running against Wendell Willkie. He's running against Adolf Hitler." On Election Day, however, the President's strongest appeal continued to be to the elements of the New Deal coalition, as, in sweeping 449 electoral votes to only 82 for Willkie, he took all but one large city, captured fourteen of fifteen key black wards, and drew especially well in low income precincts. "The New Deal," one analyst wrote afterwards, "appears to have accomplished what the Socialists, the I.W.W. and the Communists never could approach. It has drawn a class line across the map of American politics."

Roosevelt made out nearly as well in 1944. In the first wartime presidential campaign since 1864, he defeated the Republican nominee, New York's governor Thomas E. Dewey, with 432 electoral votes to only 99. Though he did not retain all of his ethnic following, certain groups proved remarkably loyal. Without the support of blacks, he would have lost both Michigan and Maryland, and in the two most Jewish wards of Boston he polled better than nine out of every ten votes. Even in 1944, in the midst of a global war, the main reason people gave for sticking with Roosevelt was: "He pulled us out of the depression."

Six months later Franklin Roosevelt was gone, but the political combination he built lived long after him. A decade after his death, a Chicago Democrat observed: "Franklin Roosevelt was the greatest precinct captain we ever had. He elected everybody—governors, senators, mayors, sheriffs, aldermen." And he continued to elect them. Every four years pundits would announce the demise of the FDR coalition, but every four years when the returns were sifted it would be clear that the Roosevelt coalition was, however modified, still potent. As recently as the 1984 campaign, an Alabama farmer, asked to explain why he was going along with Mondale, answered that he remembered the days of Herbert Hoover and was going to vote the straight Democratic ticket.

After the ballots were counted in 1984, the *New York Times*, in its lead editorial on the big Reagan victory, remarked: "Remember what commentators said in 1980 when that happened the first time? That the old New Deal coalition was dead." It added: "It's almost embarrassing to look back on that now. The old New Deal coalition, though 50 years old, remains very much alive. Look at the exit poll data on voter blocs and observe the very few among which Walter Mondale triumphed. He won the black vote, 90 percent to 9...the unemployed, 68-31...Jews, 66-32...Hispanic voters, 65-33...big-city residents, 62-36...union members, 57-41."

Yet I hardly need point out that as resilient as the Roosevelt coalition has proved to be, it fell far short of assuring a Mondale victory. If the 1984 outcome reflected historic forces from the Civil War to the Great Depression, it also revealed the impact of more recent developments. In the four decades since Roosevelt's death, numbers of Americans who were once staunch Democrats have had a change of heart. There is one man, in particular, who voted Democratic all four times FDR ran but who did not do so last year: Ronald Reagan. Though the Democrats have continued to benefit from the Roosevelt legacy, the Republicans have not spent all of the last forty years wandering in the wilderness. They have instead been fighting their way back—to such an extent that a good many people have been asking whether we are not now in the midst of a new political era in which the GOP is, and will be, as dominant as the Democrats once were, a question I shall take up in my second lecture.

TOWARD A NEW PARTY SYSTEM

For millions of Americans who identified with the Republican party, the age of Roosevelt seemed altogether incomprehensible. They could not believe that the Democrats had become the nation's new majority party because for so many decades the Republicans had seemed the country's only truly legitimate party. In his autobiography, the reformer Brand Whitlock wrote:

It was natural to be a Republican; it was more than that, it was inevitable...The Republican party was not a faction, not a group, not a wing; it was an institution...It was a fundamental and self-evident thing like life, and liberty, and the pursuit of happiness, or like the flag, or the federal judiciary. It was elemental, like gravity, the sun, the stars, the ocean. It was merely a synonym for patriotism, another name for the nation. One became...a Republican just as the Eskimo dons fur clothes. It was inconceivable that any self-respecting man should be a Democrat.

Americans of such sentiments clung to one great hope: that the string of Democratic successes under Roosevelt would prove an aberration. After all, the Democrats had enjoyed brief interludes before—under Grover Cleveland and Woodrow Wilson—and each time the country had returned to its senses. Perhaps it would do so again, and the age of FDR would prove to be only a temporary departure, especially when the Democrats could no longer count on Roosevelt as their shepherd. At the time of Roosevelt's death in 1945, and for forty years thereafter, Republicans would seize upon every scrap of evidence as a harbinger of the realignment they were sure was coming.

They could already see some promising signs even before FDR's death. Though Roosevelt had won four times, each of the last two victories had been by reduced margins. In contrast to his 1936 performance of 61 percent of the popular vote, he had received only 55 percent in 1940, less than 53 percent in 1944. So strong was opposition to FDR in 1944 in the South, especially in Texas, that it was doubtful that the section would be "Solid" for the Democrats much longer. In the North, too, Roosevelt's attraction to old-stock Americans on farms and in villages—the traditional heartland of the Republicans—had proved ephemeral, and by 1944 the GOP had largely won back the countryside.

Roosevelt also had been experiencing trouble in retaining all of his ethnic following. In 1940 numbers of German-Americans had been distressed by his hostility to their fatherland, and Irish-Americans deplored his support for their ancient enemy, England. He had also angered Italian-Americans by saying, after Mussolini invaded France, "The hand that held the dagger has stuck it in the back of its neighbor," for that remark was taken to be an ethnic slur. During World War II, Roosevelt, by associating the American cause with that of the Soviet Union, had antagonized still other groups, especially Polish-Americans in Democratic strongholds such as Detroit, Milwaukee, and Buffalo.

None of these developments, though, inspirited Republicans so much as one simple consideration: the Democrats in the postwar world would no longer have Roosevelt at the head of the ticket. If FDR in the war years did not command the following he had in 1936, no one doubted that he remained a formidable opponent. Though people of a range of political persuasions mourned his death in the spring of 1945, Republican leaders could not help but surmise that their path would be a lot easier when the incumbent of the White House was not the Great Campaigner but the much less worrisome Harry Truman.

The outcome of the first postwar elections strongly encouraged that line of speculation. So unpopular had Truman's policies become by the time of the 1946 midterm campaign that the national chairman of the Democratic party told the President to hide, and, in his place, recordings of FDR's voice were played. But to no avail. In November the Democrats suffered a shattering defeat as the Republicans regained control of Congress for the first time in sixteen years. Among the Republican newcomers were the young Californian, Richard Nixon, in the House, and in the Senate, Joseph McCarthy. So thoroughly was Truman discredited by the election that a number of prominent Democrats, led by Senator Fulbright, went so far as to suggest that the President resign from office on the spot, like a British prime minister who has lost a vote of confidence, instead of serving out the remaining two years of his term. Truman ignored that advice, and ever thereafter referred to Senator Fulbright as Senator Halfbright. Still, the 1946 elections appeared to be a turning point, a sign that the era of Democratic supremacy had died with Roosevelt and that the Republicans were regaining their former pre-eminence as the nation's majority party.

Democratic prospects in 1948, when Truman would directly confront a national electorate for the first time, seemed bleak indeed. In reply to a *Fortune* poll after the 1946 elections, only 8 percent of respondents said the next president would be a Democrat. Even that minority would have been diminished if it had known that before the 1948 contest took place, the already weakened party would suffer the loss both of a large segment of its southern wing and its radical northern wing.

Truman's difficulty with the southern wing took on serious proportions when in December 1946 he set up a President's Committee on Civil Rights. On October 29, 1947, after ten months of study, the Committee issued its historic report, "To Secure These Rights," which recommended a series of changes to break the pattern of racial discrimination and segregation. At the Democratic national convention in the summer of 1948, the young mayor of Minneapolis, Hubert Humphrey, led a successful movement to put the party on record behind a number of the Committee's proposals. That platform greatly strengthened Truman's appeal to black voters, but at a cost. Waving the battle flag of the Confederacy, the entire Mississippi delegation and thirteen of the Alabama delegates stalked out of the convention in protest.

Three days later, the bolters and their allies gathered in Birmingham to form a new party. Though the new creation bore the name of the States' Rights party, almost everyone referred to its members as the Dixiecrats. Its presidential candidate, South Carolina's governor J. Strom Thurmond, claimed to be interested primarily in the principle of states' rights, but the party was, as Ralph McGill, editor of the Atlanta *Constitution*, wrote, "really the anti-Negro party." Thurmond's running mate, Governor Fielding Wright, had made clear his views that spring when he told Mississippi blacks: "If any of you has become so deluded as to want to enter our white schools, patronize our hotels and cafes, enjoy social equality with the whites, then kindness and true sympathy require me to advise you to make your home in some state other than Mississippi." In November the Dixiecrats would deprive Truman of the electoral votes of four of the southern states.

At the same time that the Dixiecrats were undercutting Truman's following in the South, critics of his foreign policy were jeopardizing his position in northern industrial states. In September 1946 Henry Wallace had been forced out of Truman's cabinet because he had become a vocal critic of the President's "get tough" attitude toward the Soviet Union, and at the end of the next year Wallace's admirers founded a new third party, the Progressive party, which, experts believed, might pull several million votes away from Truman in November. As it turned out, the Progressives were not as great a menace to the Democrats as had been anticipated, but they may well have cost Truman the electoral votes of the large states of New York and Michigan, as well as those of Maryland.

These developments made a Republican victory in November all but certain. At the Democratic convention in July, delegates wore buttons reading, "We're just Mild about Harry," and there was even an attempt, in which FDR's sons played a prominent part, to dump Truman for another candidate. So sure were the Republicans of success that their presidential nominee, New York's governor, Thomas E. Dewey, made his bid for office, as one critic noted, with the "humorless calculation of a Certified Public Accountant in pursuit of the Holy Grail." He confined his speeches to such earthshaking statements as "Our streams should abound with fish" and "Our future lies before us."

Yet however colorless Dewey was—Alice Roosevelt Longworth said of him that "he looks like the bridegroom on a wedding cake"—everyone was certain he was going to thrash Truman in November, despite the President's "give-em-hell Harry" campaign. Two months before Election Day, Elmo Roper stopped taking polls. The heavy Dewey margin, he noted, revealed "an almost morbid resemblance to the Roosevelt-Landon figures as of about this time in 1936." Roper added, "Mr. Dewey is still so clearly ahead that we might just as well get ready to listen to his Inaugural on Jan. 20, 1949." In St.

Louis the "betting commissioner" quoted 1-15 odds that Dewey would win; in 1936 FDR had been only a 1-3 favorite. When *Newsweek* polled fifty top political writers, all fifty predicted a Dewey victory. In Washington, Democratic leaders put their homes on the market, and foreign embassies dispatched sealed diplomatic pouches carrying reports alerting their capitals to the forthcoming change of government in America.

On Election Night people settled down by their radios expecting an early bedtime since Dewey's victory statement was due not long after the polls closed. At 9 p.m., Truman was ahead, but that, commentators explained, had been foreseen; the Democrats always took a lead in the cities—the President would be snowed under when the rural areas began to report. At 10 p.m. farm regions were coming in, not as Republican as had been predicted, but still the *cognoscenti* were unperturbed. Newsboys hawked an extra of the Chigago *Tribune* with the headline: "DEWEY DEFEATS TRUMAN." But in the course of the night the mood of the "victory" celebrants at Republican headquarters in New York changed, noted one writer, from confidence to surprise, "from surprise to doubt, from doubt to disbelief, and then on to stunned fear and panic." At 4:46 a.m., *Newsweek*, which was preparing an election extra on Dewey's victory, flashed a hold-everything order to its Dayton office. By dawn, no one doubted Truman had a chance—any of three large states would be enought to give him the required total—and at breakfast, radio listeners, bleary-eyed and disbelieving, heard that Ohio was teetering. At 9:40 a.m. on a brilliantly sun-bright morning, Democratic headquarters received a call from Columbus; Truman had only a paper-thin lead, but the districts still out were in Democratic Cuyahoga County. Ohio was safe. Truman had won in the upset of the century.

The 1948 election demonstrated in convincing fashion that the Democrats were still the country's majority party. At the time, writers explained the surprising outcome by emphasizing personal attributes. Truman, they said, had aroused the country by his barnstorming, while Dewey, by his excessive caution, had "snatched defeat out of the jaws of victory." In fact, Truman had not brought an unusual number of voters to the polls (the turnout percentage was the lowest in twenty years); he won rather because he took advantage of the enduring strength of the Roosevelt coalition in an election in which balloting broke sharply on class lines. Nearly 80 percent of workers voted Democratic, a proportion higher than that any left-wing party in Europe has ever achieved. The allegiances that FDR had built in the cities were indispensable to Truman, and black ballots proved critical in several key states, including Ohio which was decided by only seven thousand votes. Truman, in sum, won chiefly because millions of Americans, fearing that a change of parties might jeopardize the gains they had made in the Roosevelt era, responded to the Democratic campaign theme song: "Don't let them take it away."

Nor was the party's triumph confined to the White House. The Democrats, who had appeared so moribund in 1946, suddenly came to life with the election of a host of men in the New Deal tradition. Among the new governors were Adlai Stevenson of Illinois and Chester Bowles of Connecticut. Minnesota voters sent to the House of Representatives for the first time from the St. Paul congressional district Eugene McCarthy. And in the Senate the crop of fresh faces included Hubert Humphrey of Minnesota; Estes Kefauver of Tennessee; Paul Douglas, a University of Chicago economics professor who had volunteered for the Marines as a private at the age of fifty, been badly wounded at Okinawa, and ended the war a major; and Lyndon B. Johnson of Texas, chosen by the tiny, and some thought suspect, margin of eighty-seven votes, a showing that earned him the ironic sobriquet of "Landslide Lyndon."

The Republicans, who had been all but guaranteed victory, had sustained a humiliating defeat. They had bought their homes in Georgetown, and now, without ever having lived in them, had to sell them. They had placed their children in posh Washington schools, and now had to withdraw them. Worst of all, they had appropriated a record quarter of a million dollars for the forthcoming inauguration and were going to have to watch the Democrats spend it. Certain of success after sixteen years out of power, they would now have to tolerate four more years of Democratic rule. "The only way a Republican will get into the White House," said Groucho Marx, "is to marry Margaret Truman."

To main-line Republicans, the election result seemed both

incomprehensible and exasperating. It was one thing to have to wait out the age of Roosevelt; FDR could be perceived to be an irresistible natural phenomenon like a typhoon. But it was quite something else to be beaten by so ordinary a fellow as Harry Truman. "I don't care how the thing is explained," Senator Taft said. "It defies all common sense for the country to send that roughneck ward politician back to the White House." The Republicans would have been even more irascible if they had been clairvoyant enough to know that the 1948 outcome was not a fluke but foretold the course of postwar American politics. Over the next generation the Democrats were no longer to have the success they had enjoyed in FDR's halcyon days. Weakened by disputes over foreign policy, fragmented by divisions over race, they would even lose some national elections. Nonetheless, the Republicans would be unable to displace them as the country's majority party.

Disappointed in 1948, Republican hopes rebounded again in 1952— and not without reason, for that year Dwight Eisenhower won an impressive victory as he swept all of the North and West. His Democratic rival, Adlai Stevenson, carried only one state outside the South, and that was a border state. Although Republicans had long been anathema below the Mason-Dixon line, Eisenhower took four former Confederate states, including Texas. Four years later, he would add Louisiana, which had been Democratic ever since 1880. Commentators, impressed by the General's ability to capture every income group and break the Democratic hold even on Catholics and union members, were still more struck by his attraction to suburban voters. Chicago's Democratic boss acknowledged, "The suburbs are murder." Analysts reasoned that as the victims of the Great Depression prospered in the postwar age and moved out of the city to greener pastures, they also shed their Democratic affiliation. Eisenhower's victory, they declared, presaged a new era of Republican supremacy.

But a closer examination of the returns indicated that these predictions were ill-founded. Despite Ike's landslide triumph in 1952, the Republicans gained only a nine-seat margin in the House and could get no better than an even split in the Senate. It required the tie-breaking vote of the Vice President of the United States, Richard Nixon, in his role as presiding officer, to permit the Republicans to organize the Senate. By 1954 the Democrats had won back control of Congress, and for six of his eight years in the White House, Eisenhower had to cope with a legislature in which the Democrats held the majority. In fact, in 1956 he became the first candidate since Zachary Taylor to win the presidency while failing to carry either house of Congress. Even in the suburbs, many of the Democrats who moved up the social scale retained their New Deal party identity. Moreover, while the Republicans held on to the old entrepreneurial middle class, the Democrats did unexpectedly well among the "new" middle class that was hospitable to government programs.

The real test of whether Eisenhower had brought about another Republican era came in 1960 when the immensely popular general was no longer on the ticket. That year the Democrats were handicapped by having a Catholic as their presidential candidate. Even though John F. Kennedy's persuasive performance before a group of Protestant ministers in Houston offset some of that disadvantage, his Catholicism hurt more than it helped. That consideration gave the Republicans an excellent opportunity to consolidate their recent gains and demonstrate that they were the majority party, especially since their candidate, Vice President Richard Nixon, had for eight years been identified with the Eisenhower administration. Nonetheless, in November Kennedy prevailed over Nixon, albeit by the smallest margin since Garfield's in 1880. In the South, Lyndon Johnson proved indispensable, especially after a rude right-wing crowd in Dallas unintentionally generated support for the Democrats by jostling Senator Johnson and Lady Bird. But the critical determinant of Kennedy's victory was the durability of the FDR coalition, even if Kennedy himself seemed removed from the passions of the New Deal era. The outcome in 1960 demonstrated that the Eisenhower presidency was merely an interruption in an age of Democratic preponderance.

In 1964 the Republicans decided upon a different strategy. There had long been a faction in the party that believed that the only reason the GOP had not done better in the past was that it had been traduced by an Eastern Establishment predisposed toward running losers such as Willkie and Dewey.

Confronted by a meaningless choice between a Democrat and a "Me Too" Republican who shared the New Deal and internationalist presumptions of the Democrats, many voters, it was said, stayed home, thereby consigning the Republicans to defeat by default. In 1964 the GOP, in nominating Barry Goldwater, promised the nation "a choice not an echo," and the Arizona senator did his best to live up to that pledge. In the Tennessee valley he suggested selling the TVA, and in criticizing the conduct of the Vietnam war, he implied that the government had become too fussy in not considering nuclear weaponry. With the intent of drawing to the polls what they assumed was a huge silent vote of conservative nationalists, the Republicans declared, "In Your Heart You Know He's Right."

The Democrats struck back by parodying such slogans and insinuating that Goldwater was peddling antiquated nostrums. To those who worried if Goldwater's hand could be trusted with the button, they said, "In Your Heart You Know He Might." Or, even more savagely, "In Your Guts You Know He's Nuts." The Democrats announced that a film was being made of Goldwater's life; it would be produced by Eighteenth Century Fox. And they insisted that Goldwater's defense policy could be summed up in one sentence: "Put your wagons in a circle."

The November returns, which the Democratic candidate, Lyndon Johnson, first saw reported on the television screens at his suite in the Hotel Driskill in Austin, set the highwater mark for the FDR coalition in the postwar era, in good part because Johnson, who had succeeded to the presidency on the assassination of John Kennedy, was determined to win office in his own right by evoking memories of Franklin Roosevelt and appealing to the same elements that had elected FDR. Johnson had first won national office in 1937 as an exponent of FDR's policies and, after achieving election to Congress in a special primary in the spring of that year as a true-blue Roosevelt man, had ridden through the streets of Galveston with his hero. In 1964 Johnson adroitly exploited the Roosevelt tradition to overwhelm Goldwater, as he captured forty-four states and a new entry in the Electoral College, the District of Columbia, to amass the biggest popular majority in American history.

The 1964 election struck the Republican party with the impact of a tidal wave. For a generation it had been a minority party. Since 1928 it had won just two Congressional elections, only one of these decisively. Now it was in the position of having lost supporters on whom they had long counted—among every ethnic group, in every social class. Blacks, once a mainstay of the GOP, voted 94 percent for Johnson. The Irish gave Johnson stronger backing than they had Kennedy. Gains among southern moderates, carefully nurtured in the Eisenhower years, were wiped out. In Knoxville bumper stickers read, "Sell TVA?— I'd Rather Sell Arizona." The Republicans even surrendered such strongholds as the state of Vermont, which had never before voted Democratic. The theory of the silent vote had been exploded, leaving the Republicans nothing but Goldwater's Arizona and some Deep South states that moved to him on the race issue. For the first time ever, the South provided the major electoral base of a GOP presidential candidate. After all of their efforts since 1945, the Republicans were not merely back where they started from but rolled all the way back to 1936.

However, 1964 turned out to be the low point in the party's fortunes. By 1966 the Republicans had already begun to rally in the midterm races that saw the election for the first time of Ronald Reagan to public office—the governorship of the country's most populous state—and ever since, though there have been peaks and valleys, the party has been climbing upwards. During Johnson's second term, the Democrats were hurt by the course of the Vietnam war—the pointless bloodletting, the runaway inflation, resentment at the violent protests—and by the white backlash against the administration's racial policies, especially after a series of long hot summers in the black ghettos.

The 1968 election showed how far the Democrats had fallen in just four years. In contrast to LBJ's 61 percent in 1964, their presidential nominee, Hubert Humphrey, a dyed-in-the-wool Roosevelt man, polled less than 43 percent. In all of the formerly Solid South, Humphrey captured only a single state—Texas, and that not because of traditional patterns but as a result of an increased turnout by blacks and Mexican-Americans. Whereas in 1936 FDR had swept all of the Great Plains, the Mountain States, and the Pacific Coast, Humphrey lost all but four states in the trans-Mississippi West. As a consequence, the expectations nurtured in 1964 of a generation-long Democratic reign were dashed, and the Democrats' arch-enemy, Richard Nixon, was installed in the White House.

Yet if the Democrats suffered grievously, there was no real evidence of a Republican realignment in 1968. So close was the contest that at NBC election headquarters, where we started our labors at 5 p.m., we went all through the night without being able to pick a winner. When at 7 a.m. we turned over the studio to Barbara Walters and Joe Garagiola for the morning news, a tiny increment of votes in a few key states could still have brought the Democrats victory. Not until noon did Humphrey concede defeat. Nixon had won by only seven-tenths of 1 percent of the popular vote, and his little more than 43 percent total in a three-way race fell far short even of a majority, let alone a realigning proportion.

In 1972 the Republicans advanced far better claims to being regarded as the country's majority party. Early in the year Nixon fretted about the likelihood that George Wallace would seize much of his turf, especially after the Alabama governor's strong showing in the primaries. But the would-be assassin's bullet that paralyzed Wallace forced him to withdraw from the race. With no strong rival on the right, Nixon was also able to occupy all of the center when the Democrats, as a consequence of a drastic reform of the nominating procedure, chose George McGovern of South Dakota as their presidential candidate. Senator McGovern had proven himself to be a man of courage on Vietnam and other issues, but he was markedly to the left of the electorate in 1972 and ran a campaign scarred with blunders and misfortune.

Hence, the outcome occasioned little surprise, except perhaps for the extent of the devastation wrought to McGovern's candidacy. Nixon took every electoral vote save those of Massachusetts and the predominantly black District of Columbia. For the first time in history, a Republican swept the entire South—in the phrase of one writer "from the Potomac to the Pedernales." Nixon's 521 electoral votes (to only 17 for McGovern) fell just two votes short of FDR's all-time high in 1936. Here at long last, surely, was the long-awaited Republican realignment.

In fact, once again appearances were deceiving. Despite the Nixon landslide, the Democrats held on to their control of both houses of Congress. Astonishingly, they even added to their margin in the United States Senate. Nor did the Republican advantage on the presidential line prove long-lived, as four years later a Democrat was elected to the White House. To be sure, Jimmy Carter barely made it, and he won only because, as a Southerner, he was able to claim the vote of every former Confederate state save Virginia. But his victory threw cold water on the claims of the Republicans to be the architects of a new political era.

The expectation of a new age of Republican supremacy, though, never died easily, and in 1980 the media once again announced that the age of FDR was over and realignment had finally been achieved. In a three-way race, Jimmy Carter got only 41 percent of the ballots, enough for just six states and the District of Columbia while Ronald Reagan received all of the rest. In addition, the Republicans captured the Senate for the first time in over a quarter of a century. On the day after the 1980 election, headline writers announced the dawn of a new political era, and a Democratic senator acknowledged, "Basically, the New Deal died yesterday."

Yet as had been true so often in the past, these pronouncements proved premature. Once more the Republicans flunked a vital test of realignment by failing to win a majority in the House. Nor did Reagan's less than 51 percent of the vote in a contest with the lowest turnout proportion in thirty-two years bear any of the telltale marks of realignment. Surveys of opinion indicated that most of Reagan's margin came from voters who did not share his conservative outlook but were displeased by Carter's leadership, especially the economy and Iran. Indeed, millions of voters, when asked which of the candidates they favored in 1980, answered, "None of the above." As one scholar noted, "Getting the electorate's feelings to stabilize long enough to produce an enduring G. O. P. majority has been harder than persuading the Loch Ness monster to stand still for a photograph."

In the 1984 election, however, the Republicans could advance much more substantial claims. Whereas in 1980 Reagan won votes that were not for him but were anti-Carter, in 1984 he got a thumping personal endorsement. Reagan won 59 percent of the ballots and took every electoral vote except those of Mondale's Minnesota and the District of Columbia. In the South, the Republicans did not confine their gains to the presidential line, but also showed strength in local races. They continued to make impressive progress in states such as North Carolina, and in Texas a Democratic pollster declared, "Our party suffered one of its worst defeats of this century."

The 1984 returns confirmed what has been growingly evident for some time: in almost every respect the Democratic Coalition has been disintegrating.

First, it has lost the Solid South. FDR in 1944 was the last Democratic presidential candidate to carry every southern state. Indeed, so much has the situation changed that Mondale failed to win a single southern state, as Reagan who had lost only Carter's Georgia in 1980, took all of the former Confederacy in 1984. Even more striking is the pattern of voting. Not since 1964 has a Democratic presidential nominee won a majority of white votes in the South. Since 1968 the Democrats have received only 24 percent of the white vote in national elections in the South, less than one in four. Nor is this racial cleavage wholly a southern phenomenon. In 1984 Reagan captured two-thirds of the ballots of white males in the country at large, including even a majority of white men making less than $5000 a year.

Second, the ethnic elements of the FDR coalition are no longer as committed as they once were. As late as 1952, the Democratic presidential nominee, Adlai Stevenson, got 56 percent of the vote of Catholics; in 1980 Carter got less than half. And in the 1984 campaign there were further signs of the fraying of ethnic support, with Jews angered by Jesse Jackson's anti-Semitic remarks and associations, and Catholics increasingly militant about abortion.

Third, the Democrats have not derived the benefits of blue collar votes to the degree that they once did. A question is often asked: If the Democrats continue to draw a higher proportion of lower income voters than the Republicans do, why are the Democrats not doing better? Four reasons: First, the blue collar worker is no longer as significant a figure as he was in the Great Depresion. In the 1950s the United States passed a significant milestone: white collar workers outnumbered blue collar for the first time. The gap between them has been widening ever since. So you can get the same percentage of miners and hod carriers you always did and not be doing nearly as well. Second, the Democrats have been losing some of their blue collar support over noneconomic issues. Since the 1960s the country has been shaken by a series of equal rights and counter culture agitations that have raised questions very different from those of the Great Depression: ERA, gay rights, abortion. "Hardhats," once loyal FDR men, mauled peace marchers and marched in Nixon parades, while other working-class voters have been drawn into the Republican camp by the right-to-life movement. Third, the Democrats require labor unions to mobilize blue collar workers, and in 1980 union members made up only half as great a proportion of the work force as they had in 1960. Fourth, and most important, many lower income citizens have simply stopped going to the polls. The dropoff has been shocking. In 1982 more than one hundred million adults did not trouble to cast ballots. And the biggest decline has come from those least well-off. If we concentrate on people with less than five years of formal education, a sure index of class, we find that in Italy, 75 percent vote; in America, 8 percent. In all the world, only one other democratic nation has so low a turnout—Botswana.

This set of developments has led analysts to raise the main question before us now: Is the historic significance of the 1984 election that it signalled the end of the Democratic age and the emergence of a new party system characterized by Republican predominance and a conservative political orientation? That conclusion seems not at all unreasonable, for no party system lasts forever; in fact, a new party system has peaked roughly every thirty-seven years. By such a measuring rod, a realignment had been due about 1968, and ever since then political historians, anticipating predictable cyclical behavior, have been in the position, as one writer has said, of "waiting for Godot" and of writing books that might well have been retitled "What to Do until the Critical Realignment Comes." Did 1984, then, reveal that the time of waiting was over, and that a new era had, at long last, arrived?

Some analysts have no doubt that this historic change has

occurred, and indeed has been manifest for quite some time. They point out that the Republicans have won four of the last five national elections, and they further note that, though political scientists persist in referring to the Democrats as the majority party, Republican presidential candidates have actually accumulated more popular votes than their opponents in postwar contests. They observe, too, that in a period when the distribution of votes in the Electoral College is tilted toward the Sunbelt, the Democrats in national elections find it hard to break out of the Rustbelt. In their view, the archetypal election was Nixon's landslide victory in 1972. That huge triumph, they say, would by now have been recognized to be the key episode in a new Republican party system, had it not been for the mischance of Watergate that permitted the Democrats to squeak through in 1976. Save for Watergate, which had no long-run electoral significance, we would now, it is said, acknowledge that we are well along in an age of substantial Republican and conservative predominance.

Though that is an argument with some force, it is not persuasive. For there are still insufficient signs that the country has been going through a massive realignment. If we are already in a new Republican era, how does one account for the fact that over two-thirds of the governorships in the country are held by Democrats, not Republicans? How, furthermore, does it happen that most of the members of the House of Representatives sit on the Democratic, not the Republican, side of the aisle? And that in the 1984 elections the Democrats actually picked up two seats in the United States Senate? The Democrats, too, control most county governments, most state legislatures, twice as many city halls as the Republicans. Reagan's victory was more a personal one than a vindication either for his views or his party, and it is by no means clear that Republican success will outlive the President. "Is it possible that Ronald Reagan is going to serve a two-term presidency that does no lasting good for the GOP?" asked an editor for the *Washington Post*. "Yes it is. It seems more and more likely that Reagan's personalized presidency will come to resemble Dwight D. Eisenhower's—which ushered in eight years of Democratic rule."

Not since the age of Roosevelt has any party won three

successive presidential elections, and it is far from certain that the Republicans will be able to better that record in 1988. One historian has written: "As the glow of last month's victory fades, Republicans might find themselves reflecting with Wellington that 'nothing except a battle lost can be half so melancholy as a battle won.' The dark side for the GOP is that the party must now govern during four perilous years with a lame duck (and perhaps faltering) president, a hostile House of Representatives and a Senate majority imperiled in 1986. Tack on an impending struggle over President Reagan's successor and the Republicans will be pressed to retain the White House in 1988, despite sweeping 49 states this fall."

Nonetheless, the situation today is brighter for the Republicans than it has been at any time in the past, because of one crucial consideration. No longer do a majority of those who identify with a political party incline toward the Democrats. About as many party identifiers now call themselves Republicans. Moreover, much of this gain for the GOP has come from first-time voters who are the building blocks of any realignment. For a long time the Democrats had been able to count on the allegiance of the youngest voters. As recently as 1980, when Reagan was sweeping most of the country, young people were preponderantly for Carter. But in 1984 they not only went overwhelmingly for Reagan, the oldest incumbent ever in the White House, but also were disposed to vote Republican in Congressional races and, most significantly, to identify themselves as Republicans rather than Democrats. There is then a potential now, as there has not been in the past, for the emergence of the Republicans as the new majority party.

That scenario is still, however, not the most likely one. The most important feature of political behavior in recent years has not been realignment but rather the remarkable growth in the number of people with no party attachment. From 1952 to 1980 the proportion of the electorate that does not identify strongly with either political party rose from one-fifth to one-third. That figure means that, overwhelmingly, the distribution of ballots is still determined by the historic forces I have been describing, for nearly two-thirds of the voters are party identifiers. But the more than one-third independent segment is sizeable enough not merely to determine the outcome of an election but to turn a close contest into a landslide.

What has caused this party decomposition? We are not altogether sure. There are, though, some suggestive data and several informed guesses. We know that the falloff has been greatest among Southern whites who, unhappy with the civil rights stands of the national Democratic party, have not been able to bring themselves to move altogether into the ranks of the Republicans. The decline in party identification, we believe, may well be related to the influence of the mass media, especially television, toward making party seem less pertinent and personalities of candidates more salient. It is also almost certainly connected to the explosion in higher education (with the number of college graduates rising fivefold in one generation), for going to college severs many young people from ties of family and community and encourages the conviction that parties are not required as intermediaries. It very likely has something to do, too, with the considerable augmentation of the middle class, a phenomenon that serves to attenuate traditional working-class ties to party. That circumstance is also often accompanied by geographical mobility—as in the movement from inner city to suburb—which is further dislocating. Finally, it probably derives from the ascendancy of single issue movements that makes a cause like the abortion amendment seem more vital than party affiliation.

Important though they are, these trends do not necessarily persuade a voter to change parties. To be sure, as a Democratic voter rises in the social order he or she may gravitate to the Republicans. But, as has been noted, it is not easy to change party affiliation; it can be as painful as changing one's religion. Hence, many Americans are what psychologists call "conflicted." They are tugged between their original party identification and the pull of new experiences. In the end, they may be less likely to switch parties than to refuse to identify with any party.

Consequently, we should be wary of accepting the notion that even Reagan's mammoth victory in 1984 signified the arrival of the realignment that, like Godot, has so long been awaited. The Republican successes have the potential to be that, but only the potential. It seems more likely that the decline of party identification means that we are in a period when political

37

contests will be much more volatile than they have been in the past; when the emergence of new personalities may shift the allegiance of the public from party to party in rapid order; and when the hand of History will rest more gently on the electorate than it ever has before.

A NOTE ON SOURCES

The best overview of electoral behavior is James L. Sundquist, *Dynamics of the Party System* (1973), but William Nesbit Chambers and Walter Dean Burnham, eds., *The American Party Systems* (1967); Robert A. Kelley, *The Cultural Patterns in American Politics* (1979); and Everett C. Ladd, *American Political Parties* (1970) are also of value. No one uses a term such as "realignment" without recognizing an enormous debt to V. O. Key, Jr., whose posthumous volume, with Milton C. Cummings, Jr., *The Responsible Electorate* (1966) contends that voting is more rational than some writers have implied. The element of ethnicity is dealt with in John M. Allswang, *A House for All Peoples* (1971); Mark R. Levy and Michael S. Kramer, *The Ethnic Factor* (1972); and Lawrence Fuchs, *The Political Behavior of American Jews* (1956). For late nineteenth-century political behavior, see Paul M. Kleppner, *The Cross of Culture* (1970); Richard J. Jensen, *Winning the Midwest* (1971); and Walter Dean Burnham, *Presidential Ballots: 1838-1892*. The New Deal coalition is analyzed in Samuel Lubell, *The Future of American Politics* (1951), Kristi Anderson, *The Creation of a Democratic Majority, 1928-1936* (1979), and Paul F. Lazarsfeld, Bernard Berelson, and Hazel Gaudet, *The People's Choice* (1948). For post-New Deal developments, see Everett Carll Ladd, Jr., with Charles D. Hadley, *Transformations of the American Party System* (1975), and the pioneering work of the Survey Research Center at Michigan, especially Angus Campbell et al., *The American Voter* (1960). Other important studies include John H. Fenton, *Midwest Politics* (1966); John R. Petrocik, *Party Coalitions* (1981); Seymour Martin Lipset, ed., *Party Coalitions in the 1980s* (1981); Walter Dean Burnham, *The Current Crisis in American Politics* (1982); and Jeff Fishel, ed., *Parties and Elections in an Anti-Party Age* (1978). In *Mediacracy* (1975), Kevin Phillips expresses second thoughts about the ideas he advanced in *The Emerging Republican Majority* (1969). The dissolution of parties is treated in Martin P. Wattenberg, *The Decline of American Political Parties, 1952-1980* (1984); William Crotty, *American Parties in Decline* (1980); and in David S. Broder's 1972 volume whose title says it all: *The Party's Over.*

WILLIAM E. LEUCHTENBURG

Professor Leuchtenburg was born on September 28, 1922, in Ridgewood, New York. He received the B.A. degree from Cornell University in 1943 and the M.A. and Ph.D. degrees from Columbia University in 1944 and 1951 respectively. He taught for brief periods at New York University, Smith College, and Harvard before going back to Columbia where he remained for over thirty years (1952-1983). For his excellence as teacher and scholar, Columbia named him De Witt Clinton Professor of History. Since 1983 Professor Leuchtenburg has been the William Rand Kenañ, Jr. Professor of History at the University of North Carolina, Chapel Hill.

In addition to his primary teaching duties at Columbia and North Carolina, he has lectured at seventeen foreign universities in Canada, England (including the Harmsworth Lectures at Oxford), Scotland, Wales, Austria, Italy, and Israel. Over fifty-five universities in the United States have invited him for special lectures. He has also held senior fellowships in the Center for Advanced Study in the Behavioral Sciences at Stanford, the Inter-University Consortium for Political Research, Ann Arbor, Michigan, the National Endowment for the Humanities, the Guggenheim Foundation, the National Humanities Center, the Mellon Foundation, and the Woodrow Wilson Center for International Affairs.

Professor Leuchtenburg has written eight books on twentieth-century America:

> Flood Control Politics (1953);
>
> The Perils of Prosperity, 1914-32 (1958; translated into Japanese);
>
> Franklin D. Roosevelt and the New Deal, 1932-1940 (1963; winner of the Bancroft Prize and the Francis Parkman Prize; translated into Italian and Japanese);
>
> New Deal and Global War (1964);
>
> The Great Age of Change (1964);
>
> A Trouble Feast (1973);
>
> War and Social Change in Twentieth Century America (1977); and
>
> In the Shadow of FDR: From Harry Truman to Ronald Reagan (1983).

In addition Professor Leuchtenburg is co-author of three books and editor of seven others. He has also contributed eighteen chapters to books of collected essays, and published thirty articles in both scholarly and popular journals. He is currently under contract to

Oxford University Press to write the final volume in *The Oxford History of the United States* and another book centering on Franklin D. Roosevelt and the Supreme Court crisis of 1937.

Professor Leuchtenburg has served as editorial consultant for seventeen scholarly journals and projects and has contributed his expertise as consultant, advisor, director, committeeman, trustee, etc. to some thirty other projects and programs. And, in addition, he has carried his full share of committee assignments at Columbia and North Carolina.

In recognition of his outstanding contributions to the field of history, his fellow historians have elected him to many places of honor and responsibility in the historical profession including the presidency of the Society of American Historians and the Organization of American Historians.

Previous
CHARLES EDMONDSON HISTORICAL LECTURES

1977-78

Paul K. Conkin, *American Christianity in Crisis*: "Religious Rationalism—God without a Redeemer" and "Darwinism—Nature without a Creator" (Baylor University Press)

1979-80

Walter LaFeber, *The Third Cold War*: "The Kissinger Response" and "The Carter Response" (Baylor University Press)

1980-81

Martin E. Marty, *Religious Crises in Modern America*: "The Modernist Attraction, 1880-1925" and "The Fundamentalist Attraction, 1925-1980" (Baylor University Press)

1981-82

William H. McNeill, *The Great Frontier: Freedom and Hierarchy in Modern Times* (Princeton University Press)

1982-83

Robert L. Heilbroner, "Capitalism in Transition: The Twenty-first Century"

1983-84

C. Vann Woodward, "Continuing Themes in Southern History: The Strange Career of Jim Crow, 1954-1984" and "The Burden of Southern History, 1952-1984"